TINY TERRORS

BLUE-RINGED OCTOPUSES

JILL KEPPELER

PowerKiDS press

Published in 2024 by The Rosen Publishing Group, Inc.
2544 Clinton Street, Buffalo, NY 14224

Portions of this work were originally authored by Daisy Allyn and published as *Deadly Blue-Ringed Octopuses*. All new material in this edition was authored by Jill Keppeler.

Editor: Dwayne Hicks
Book Design: Michael Flynn

Photo Credits: Cover, pp. 11, 17 Thierry Eidenweil/Shutterstock.com; (series background) Ruswantodarkness/Shutterstock.com; p. 5 Divelvanov/Shutterstock.com; p. 7 kaschibo/Shutterstock.com; p. 8 Sahara Frost/Shutterstock.com; p. 9 K.Pock Pics/Shutterstock.com; p. 13 rudy tulang/Shutterstock.com; p. 15 Ethan Daniels/Shutterstock.com; p. 18 Sukpaiboonwat/Shutterstock.com; p. 19 Sascha Janson/Shutterstock.com; p. 21 Mike Workman/Shutterstock.com.

Cataloging-in-Publication Data

Names: Keppeler, Jill.
Title: Blue-Ringed octopuses / Jill Keppeler
Description: New York : Powerkids Press, 2024. | Series: Tiny terrors | Includes index, glossary, and bibliographic information
Identifiers: ISBN 9781642826241 (pbk) | ISBN 9781642826258 (library bound) | ISBN 9781642826265 (ebook)
Subjects: LCSH: Octopuses– Juvenile literature | Poisonous animals–Juvenile literature
Classification: LCC QL430.3 O2 K47 2023 | DDC 594.56–dc2

Manufactured in the United States of America

CPSIA Compliance Information: Batch #CSPK24. For Further Information contact Rosen Publishing at 1-800-237-9932.

CONTENTS

TINY AND TERRIBLE

Many blue-ringed octopuses are only the size of a golf ball—but they pack a big punch! These tiny terrors are some of most deadly examples of the more than 300 species, or kinds, of octopuses. These creatures are cephalopods. This group also includes squid and cuttlefish.

All octopuses have eight arms. In fact, their name means "eight feet." They all have a large head and soft body. However, they can also range from 2 inches (5 cm) to 18 feet (5.5 m) long!

DEADLY DETAILS

Octopuses have three hearts and blue blood. Their blood is this color because it's based in copper instead of iron like human blood.

Octopuses have **suction cups** on their arms. They use these to hold their prey, or the animals they hunt.

DANGER SIGNS

If you see a blue-ringed octopus by itself, you might be surprised. Where are the blue rings? These octopuses are usually a yellowish-brown color. They have darker spots and bumpy skin. These colors help them hide on the ocean floor.

However, if they are scared or bothered, bright blue and black circles will show up on their body. The circles almost look like they're glowing. These colors tell other animals (including humans) to be careful!

DEADLY DETAILS

These blue rings are a type of aposematism. This means animals use their bright colors as a warning to predators that they have poison or don't taste good.

Some animals that use aposematism wear their bright colors all the time. Blue-ringed octopuses only get bright when they're bothered.

DIFFERENT TYPES

There are a few different kinds of blue-ringed octopuses. Two of them are the greater and the lesser blue-ringed octopuses. The "greater" octopus has bigger rings. The "lesser" species is bigger in general and is more common. Their rings are usually about 0.08 inch (2 mm) across.

DEADLY DETAILS

Blue-ringed octopuses are in the **genus** *Hapalochlaena*. The greater blue-ringed octopus is *Hapalochlaena lunulate*. The lesser blue-ringed octopus is *Hapalochlaena maculosa*.

Hapalochlaena maculosa

A tidal pool is a small pocket of ocean water that's left behind, usually along a rocky coast, when the tide goes out.

These types of octopuses live in **shallow**, warm waters in the Indian and Pacific Oceans from Australia to Japan. They may live in **coral reefs** and tidal pools.

SHOWING THEIR COLORS

Blue-ringed octopuses show off their colors when alarmed. But how do they do this? They have thousands of special cells called chromatophores just under their skin. These cells let them change color very quickly. Many octopuses have these cells.

There are also special chromatophores called iridophores. These iridophores **reflect** light and make the blue rings **iridescent**. When upset, the octopuses use their **muscles** to show these cells under the regular chromatophores. That makes up their bright blue rings.

Octopuses don't want to attack people. They want to stay away from them. Their bright coloring is a clear warning.

OCTO BOD

Like all octopuses, the blue-ringed octopus has eight **flexible** arms with suction cups. It has no bones at all. In fact, its body is like a big sack, or bag. The head isn't very separated from the body, and the body is very soft. Because of this and the lack of bones, octopuses can **squeeze** themselves into some very small spaces!

They have big eyes and a mouth on the underside of their head. This mouth has a beak the octopus can use to break its prey's shell.

DEADLY DETAILS

Although their body is very soft, octopuses are really about 90 percent muscle!

If an octopus loses an arm, it can regrow it. As soon as one arm is cut off, the growth of a new arm will start.

AN OCTOPUS'S LIFE

Some baby blue-ringed octopuses are only about the size of a pea when they **hatch**. They grow up quickly and have short lives, only about two years. These octopuses only mate, or come together to make babies, once in their lives.

Males die after mating. Females will lay about 50 to 100 tiny eggs. They'll carry and guard these eggs for about 50 days. They won't eat the whole time! They die after the eggs hatch.

DEADLY DETAILS

Blue-ringed octopuses are nocturnal. This means that they're active at night.

A mother blue-ringed octopus will carry her eggs under one of her arms.

DEADLY SPIT

Although it's tiny and looks kind of cute, the blue-ringed octopus can be one of the most dangerous animals on Earth. It makes two kinds of venom, or poison, in its body. One, it uses to hunt its prey. The other is for self-defense, or protecting itself.

This venom is in their saliva, or spit. They have some of the deadliest venom in the world! In fact, one bite has enough venom to kill about 25 people.

DEADLY DETAILS

Venom is a toxin, or poison, that an animal puts into its prey or a predator by biting or stinging. The blue-ringed octopus's venom also serves as poison if an animal eats it.

A blue-ringed octopus's venom is far stronger than the venom of any land animal.

WHAT'S FOR DINNER?

Blue-ringed octopuses eat small crabs and shrimp. The octopus bites its prey and makes a hole in its shell. After it uses its venom to kill the prey, it eats up the insides. Sometimes, a blue-ringed octopus just lets some of its venom go into the water and waits for it to affect its prey. Then it's dinner time!

These octopuses will also eat small fish if they can catch them. This usually only happens if a fish is injured, or hurt, already.

shrimp

Blue-ringed octopuses will pounce, or jump quickly, on their prey and grab it with their arms.

STAY AWAY!

Blue-ringed octopuses are shy and good at hiding. Still, if they think they're in danger, they'll bite. This bite usually doesn't hurt at all, and a person might not even know they've been bitten.

As the venom spreads, however, they'll become paralyzed, which means they can't move. They'll stop breathing, and if they don't get help fast, they'll die! There are no medicines, or drugs, to help. The person will need a machine to help them keep breathing until the venom goes away.

DEADLY DETAILS

Octopuses don't want to bite people—they want to stay away from them! They'll flatten their body and stay still if a human is nearby.

These octopuses are small and have bright colors, so people will sometimes pick them up for photos. They don't know the danger they're in!

GLOSSARY

coral reef: The hard remains of coral animals that form a line in ocean waters.

flexible: Able to bend easily.

genus: The scientific name for a group of plants or animals that share most features.

hatch: To break open or come out of.

iridescent: Shining with different colors.

muscle: A part of the body that produces motion.

reflect: To throw back light, heat, or sound without absorbing it, or taking it in.

shallow: Not deep.

squeeze: To move into a small space.

suction cup: One of the circular parts on octopuses' arms that grab onto prey.

FOR MORE INFORMATION

BOOKS

Drimmer, Stephanie. *Ink! 100 Fun Facts About Octopuses, Squid, and More.* Washington, D.C.: National Geographic Kids, 2019.

Murray, Julie. *Blue-Ringed Octopus*. Minneapolis, MN: Abdo Zoom, 2021.

WEBSITES

Blue-Ringed Octopus
www.dkfindout.com/uk/animals-and-nature/squid-snails-and-shellfish/blue-ringed-octopus/
DK Find Out! offers facts about these tiny terrors.

Octopuses
www.nationalgeographic.com/animals/invertebrates/facts/octopus-facts
Learn more about octopuses in general from National Geographic.

INDEX